RUM PUNCH

An exclusive edition for

for all your gift books and gift stationery

This edition first published in Great Britain in 2019
by Allsorted Ltd, Watford, Herts, UK WD19 4BG

© Susanna Geoghegan Gift Publishing

Author: Michael Powell
Cover design: Milestone Creative
Contents design: seagulls.net

ISBN: 978-1-912295-92-0

Printed in China

RUM PUNCH

A KNOCK-OUT SPIRIT TO GIVE YOU A LIFT

RUM

(NOUN): AN ALCOHOLIC SPIRIT FERMENTED FROM MOLASSES OR SUGARCANE JUICE AND DISTILLED.

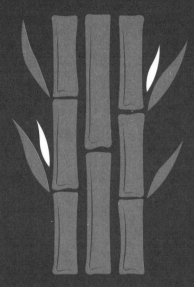

WHAT IS RUM?

Rum is an alcoholic drink made from molasses or from sugarcane juice by fermentation and distillation. The distillate is then bottled immediately to produce a mild and clean-tasting clear rum, or aged in oak barrels – sometimes for decades – where it acquires an amber to deep brown colour, and a more complex flavour.

ORIGIN OF RUM

The origin of the word *rum* is uncertain. It may have arisen from the last syllable for the Latin word *saccharum* (sugar); or an old British slang term for 'the best', as in 'having a rum time'; or by shortening words like rumbullion or rumbustion; or even the Romany word *rum* (strong). Rum is also the Turkish name for Greeks: some of the earliest rum distillers were Greek Christians in the eastern Mediterranean.

TODAY I LEARNED HOW TO BAKE MEAN BANANA BREAD. THE SECRET, APPARENTLY, IS HALF A CUP OF DARK RUM.

Adele Griffin

FIRST DISTILLATION

Precursors to rum date back to ancient India and China, and in the fourteenth century, Venetian merchant and explorer Marco Polo described drinking a 'very good wine of sugar' in the area that became modern-day Iran. In 1536, Dutch businessman Erasmus Schetz established the first commercial distillery in Brazil, using the by-products from sugar production. Within a hundred years, there were about 350 stills operating in the country. The first distillation of rum in the Caribbean took place in the early 1600s using molasses and Dutch distilling technology, but today, rum is produced internationally, although the Caribbean remains the biggest producer (80% of the world's rum is made there) and most of its sugar cane comes from Puerto Rico. However, for rum consumption, the biggest market is India.

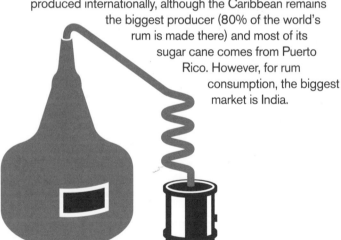

I WANT SIXTEEN PINTS OF RUM AND THEN I GO 'BOM BOM'.

Sam and the Womp

THE DOG AT FIFTEEN CASHES IN WITHOUT THE AID OF RUM OR GIN. THE MODEST, SOBER, BONE-DRY HEN LAYS EGGS FOR NOGGS AND DIES AT 10. BUT SINFUL, GINFUL, RUM-SOAKED MEN SURVIVE THREE-SCORE YEARS AND TEN.

Charles Gavan Duffy

HOW TO MAKE A
DAIQUIRI

This classic cocktail is thought to have been invented in Cuba by an American mining engineer called Jennings Cox at the turn of the twentieth century, and it is probably named after a beach and iron mine near Santiago de Cuba. The drink became very popular in the US during the Second World War when whiskey and vodka were rationed, but Latin American rum was still available.

Ingredients:
50ml white rum
1 ½ tbsp freshly squeezed lime juice
1 tbsp sugar syrup or caster sugar
Shaved ice
Wedge of lime

Fill a cocktail shaker with ice, then add the rum, lime juice and sugar syrup, and shake well. Strain into a chilled cocktail glass and garnish with a wedge of lime.

The Daiquiri was the favourite drink of President John F Kennedy and Ernest Hemingway. A Hemingway Daiquiri (aka *papa doble*) uses 100ml rum, the juice of two limes and half a grapefruit, six drops of maraschino liqueur and no sugar.

||||||||||||||||||||||||||||||||||||||||||||||||||||||||||||||||||||||||||||||||||||||||||||||||||||||||||||||||||

TYPES OF RUM

Today, rum is produced in more than 80 countries, using different ingredients (sugar/molasses/sugar cane juice), methods of fermentation and distillation, blending styles and ageing techniques. Rum can be drunk straight and/or with water/soda/ice or used in a wide range of famous cocktails.

White rum: clear and has a mild flavour, usually aged for one or two years, then filtered to remove the colour.

Gold rum: amber/gold, usually aged for several years in oak barrels and has a stronger flavour profile.

Dark rum: dark orange/deep brown, aged for several years to decades (or may just have artificial colouring) and has robust flavours.

Black rum: very dark and sweet, often aged in charred barrels and retains some of the molasses.

Navy (or Navy-style) rum: traditional dark, full-bodied blended rum associated with the British Royal Navy and with British territories including Guyana, Jamaica, Barbados and Trinidad.

Premium aged rum: the finest and most expensive matured rum, dark coloured and often blended.

Vintage rum: bottled from specific vintage years of production, which appears on the label.

Overproof: has an ABV of above 57%.

Spiced rum: rum flavoured with spices, seeds, dried fruit extracts, root, leaf or bark of edible flora.

Cachaça: full-flavoured Brazilian sugar cane spirit (the national drink of Brazil), made from fresh sugar cane juice, with little to no ageing.

Rhum Agricole: fermented and distilled from pure, fresh cane juice, made principally in the French territories of the Caribbean, especially Martinique (which has the Appellation d'Origine Contrôlée mark).

THERE IS A RUM FOR EVERYONE, BUT THEY DON'T KNOW IT ... YET.

Erik Voskamp

REASSURINGLY EXPENSIVE: HALL OF FAME

Appleton Estate's 50-year-old Jamaican rum was bottled from a blend of rums, which had been aged in hand-selected oak barrels for a minimum of 50 years and were from pre-1962-independence. Only 800 bottles were produced, and they sell today for about US$6,000 each.

RUM AND SLAVERY

The invention and manufacture of Caribbean rum was made possible by slavery. Slaves planted and fertilised the sugar cane, cut the stalks and took them to the mill where they were crushed to collect the juice. This water was then boiled away to leave sugar crystals and a thick syrupy by-product – molasses. At first, the molasses were used as a sweetener, but subsequently they were distilled to produce rum.

A RUM AND PEPSI IS JUST NOT THE SAME AS A RUM AND COKE®.

Bill Thornton

THE PROBLEM, RIGHT, BETWEEN RUM AND GIN, IS THAT GIN, RIGHT, IT LEADS TO THE MELANCHOLY. WHEREAS RUM INCITES VIOLENCE, IT ALSO ALLOWS YOU TO BE LIBERATED FROM YOUR SELF-DOUBT.

Alfie Solomons (Tom Hardy), *Peaky Blinders*

HOW TO MAKE A MAI TAI

Two men claim to have invented this cocktail. The first is Victor Bergeron, who opened his first Polynesian restaurant in Oakland, San Francisco, USA in 1934, and created the drink during the Second World War for some friends from Tahiti; one of them exclaimed, 'Mai tai-roa aé' ('out of this world'), and the name stuck. The second claimant is Ernest Gantt (aka Donn Beach), who ran a beachcomber-themed restaurant in Hollywood during the 1930s, where he created the Original Beachcomber Rum Concoction (Mai Tai), along with other rum-based cocktails such as the Zombie (see page 29) and Missionary's Downfall (see page 60).

Ingredients:
40ml rum
20ml orange Curaçao
30ml freshly squeezed lime
10ml orgeat (almond) syrup
10ml sugar syrup
Shaved ice
Fresh mint leaves
Wedge of lime

Mix all of the ingredients in a shaker and shake well. Strain into a glass filled with crushed ice, garnish with fresh mint and a wedge of lime.

UM, UM, UM. STOP THAT THUNDER! PLENTY TOO MUCH THUNDER UP HERE. WHAT'S THE USE OF THUNDER? UM, UM, UM. WE DON'T WANT THUNDER; WE WANT RUM; GIVE US A GLASS OF RUM. UM, UM, UM!

Herman Melville

REASSURINGLY EXPENSIVE:
HALL OF FAME

In 2011, Mark Lascelles and his colleague Andy Langshaw were performing an inventory of the old wines and spirits in the cellars of Harewood House, a country house near Leeds, West Yorkshire, UK. The house was built in the eighteenth century by Henry Lascelles, who made his fortune in the West Indies as an entrepreneur and slave trader, so maybe it wasn't so surprising that the two men should stumble across a collection of dirty, mouldy, old bottles that contained Harewood Rum dating back to 1780, and represented the single oldest batch of rum in existence. The last 16 bottles sold at auction for more than £100,000, and the proceeds were donated to the Geraldine Connor Foundation, which promotes equality and diversity by bringing people together through arts and culture.

WINE IS CRYING JUICE. RUM IS WORSE.

Retta

THE TRIANGLE TRADE

Rum and molasses were an important part of the triangle trade, which relied on slavery for its production and was also traded in exchange for slaves. From the mid-sixteenth century until the 1807 abolition of slavery, throughout the British Empire, thousands of ships departed from England loaded with goods such as copper, cloth, fur and beads, bound for Africa, where they would be traded for slaves. The slaves were then transported to the West Indies on the infamous Middle Passage, where they were exchanged for money and labour-intensive goods from the New World colonies such as rum and molasses, hemp and tobacco, which were then transported back to England.

BEFORE AN ATTACK WHO CAN SAY ANYTHING THAT GIVES YOU THE MOMENTARY WELL-BEING THAT RUM DOES? THE ONLY TIME IT ISN'T GOOD FOR YOU IS WHEN YOU WRITE OR WHEN YOU FIGHT.

Ernest Hemingway

THERE'S ONE **WHITE POWDER** WHICH IS BY FAR THE MOST LETHAL KNOWN, **IT'S CALLED SUGAR ...** THE CARIBBEAN BACK IN THE EIGHTEENTH CENTURY WAS A SOFT DRUG PRODUCER: **SUGAR, RUM, TOBACCO, CHOCOLATE.** AND IN ORDER TO DO IT, THEY HAD TO ENSLAVE AFRICANS.

Noam Chomsky

> DON'T DIE OF LOVE: IN HEAVEN
> ABOVE OR HELL. THEY'LL NOT
> ENDURE YOU: WHY LOOK SO GLUM
> WHEN DOCTOR RUM IS WAITING
> FOR TO CURE YOU?
>
> Oliver Herford

THE WORLD'S STRONGEST

Scotch Malt Whisky Society's R5.1 Long Pond 9-year-old single cask Jamaican rum is 81.3% ABV. Even though only 525 bottles were made, you can pick one up for less than £50. The tasting notes on the bottle say, 'Mint humbugs. A tropical swimming pool. Plastic flip-flops and wicker loungers, followed by pumpkin-seed oil, damson vinegar and Cola-cubes. With real Cola (and pressed lime) it was sublime!'

RIVER ANTOINE
ROYALE GRENADIAN RUM

One of the oldest still in existence, this rum has the distinction of being manufactured in exactly the same way it was back in the 1700s, in the same place (in the north of the West Indian island of Grenada) and using much of the same equipment. Local sugar cane is crushed using a big old water wheel powered by the River Antoine, then the cane juice runs down open-air wooden guttering to reach the boiling house. After boiling, the liquor is ladled by hand into large stone fermentation tanks. No yeast is added because the process relies on local airborne yeast. After ten days of fermentation, the distilled rum is hand-pumped into bottles. The rum is 69% ABV, and some aficionados say it tastes like lighter fluid.

ON OUR HONEYMOON WE TALKED AND TALKED. WE STAYED IN A BEACHFRONT VILLA, AND WE DRANK RUM AND LEMONADE AND TALKED SO MUCH THAT I NEVER EVEN NOTICED WHAT COLOUR THE SEA WAS.

Chris Cleave

27

REASSURINGLY EXPENSIVE: HALL OF FAME

Pyrat Rum's Cask 1623 is a blend of nine Caribbean pot still rums, some of which have been aged for up to forty years. Its tasting notes include honey, caramel, orange and apricot. It also has some nice vanilla accents, with some spicy tobacco underneath. Each unique hand-blown bottle bears an image of Hoti, the patron saint of bartenders, and is presented in a walnut box and costs about £250.

HOW TO MAKE A ZOMBIE

This recipe uses 65ml of rum, one of which is high-proof Bacardi 151 (75.5% ABV/151 proof) plus brandy, so the Zombie earns its name.

Ingredients:
1½ tsp Bacardi 151
25ml white rum
25ml dark rum
10ml apricot brandy
50ml freshly squeezed lime juice
150ml pineapple juice
Orange juice
1 tsp grenadine syrup
Ice
Maraschino cherries
Orange slices

Mix the brandy and the light and dark rum in a cocktail shaker with ice, then add the lime and pineapple juices. Strain into a highball glass filled with crushed ice, add the grenadine then top up with orange juice. Float the Bacardi on top, and garnish with a cherry and orange slice.

IF I EVER GO MISSING, PLEASE PUT MY PHOTO ON A RUM BOTTLE, NOT A MILK CARTON. I WANT MY FRIENDS TO KNOW I AM MISSING!

Laurie Manzer

A TOT OF RUM

Rum has always been associated with pirates, but really this applied to all sailors from the seventeenth century onwards. Three main types of drink were stored onboard during long voyages: water (which was drunk first, because it quickly went rancid), beer (which also became undrinkable after several weeks) and rum (which could remain potable for months). The Royal Navy changed the daily ration from brandy to rum in 1655 with the capture of the island of Jamaica. Sailors originally received two-thirds of a pint of rum each day, and from 1756, lemon juice was added to prevent scurvy.

WHY IS THE RUM GONE?

Jack Sparrow, *Pirates of the Caribbean: The Curse of the Black Pearl*

HOW TO MAKE BUMBO

Pirates mixed their rum with water, sugar and nutmeg or cinnamon to make a drink they called Bumbo. In this recipe, the lemon juice is kinder on the modern palate, and is a nod to the sailors of the British Royal Navy.

Ingredients:
50ml dark rum
25ml lemon juice
1 tsp grenadine syrup
¼ tsp (grated) nutmeg

Half fill a cocktail shaker with ice cubes, combine the ingredients and shake. Then strain into a cocktail glass, with a sugared rim.

32

SAILORS WILL NEVER BE CONVINCED THAT RUM IS A DANGEROUS THING, BY TAKING IT AWAY FROM THEM, AND GIVING IT TO THE OFFICERS: NOR THAT, THAT TEMPERANCE IS THEIR FRIEND, WHICH TAKES FROM THEM WHAT THEY HAVE ALWAYS HAD, AND GIVES THEM NOTHING IN THE PLACE OF IT.

Richard Henry Dana Jr.

||||||||||||||||||||||||||||||||||||||||||||||||||||||||||||||||||||||||||||||||||||||||||||||||||||||||||||||

> FIFTEEN MEN ON THE DEAD MAN'S CHEST –
> YO-HO-HO, AND A BOTTLE OF RUM!
> DRINK AND THE DEVIL HAD DONE FOR THE
> REST – YO-HO-HO, AND A BOTTLE OF RUM!
>
> Robert Louis Stevenson

REASSURINGLY EXPENSIVE: HALL OF FAME

In 1887, Homère Clément purchased an ailing 43-acre sugar plantation known as Domaine de l'Acajou on the island of Martinique. He used it to pioneer the Rhum Agricole method of rum production (from sugarcane juice), which is based on the distillery methods of the great Armagnacs of southwestern France. His Rhum Clément company still produces world-class rum today and a bottle of Rhum Clément Vieux Vintage 1952 will set you back about £1,000.

MAY YOUR ANCHOR BE TIGHT, YOUR CORK BE LOOSE, YOUR RUM BE SPICED, AND YOUR COMPASS BE TRUE.

Anon

'MYFANWY SAYS YOU DRINK TOO MUCH RUM. I THINK SHE WAS RIGHT.'

'IT'S MY AFTERSHAVE.'

'WELL, THEN, YOU DRINK TOO MUCH AFTERSHAVE.'

Malcolm Pryce

THE WORLD'S STRONGEST

Denros Strong Rum (80% ABV) is one of the strongest rums in the world, and has been produced on St. Lucia since 1932. It was originally produced by the Barnard family at their Dennery Distillery, and now by St. Lucia Distillers.

GROG

Watered-down rum was called grog, after 'Old Grog', the reputed nickname of British Admiral Vernon (1684–1757). Vernon wore an old grogram cloak, and on 21st August 1740, introduced the order that rum should be offered to British sailors watered down, to lessen drunkenness. The ration was eventually reduced from two-thirds of a pint to a daily 'tot' – one-eighth of an imperial pint (71ml) of rum at 95.5 proof (which in those days was 54.5% ABV) – until the practice was abolished on 31st July 1970 (aka 'Black Tot Day').

REASSURINGLY EXPENSIVE:
HALL OF FAME

Bacardi Paraiso is part of The Facundo Rum Collection. This collection is a limited-edition range of four aged sipping rums made from the Bacardi family's personal reserves, which pays homage to the company's founder Don Facundo Bacardi Massó. Paraiso is aged for up to 23 years and finished in Cognac casks, and each hand-numbered bottle costs about US$250. Paraiso's nose combines vanilla, shortbread, ginger, oak, cherry, marzipan, salted caramel and hazelnut; the flavour notes include all of these plus creamy milk chocolate and raisin.

HOW TO MAKE A PIÑA COLADA

The invention of this classic Puerto Rican cocktail has been attributed to Ramon Marrero, a bartender at the Caribe Hilton in 1954, but in the nineteenth century, the Puerto Rican pirate Roberto Cofresi is said to have boosted the morale of his crew with a cocktail using the same ingredients. National Piña Colada day is celebrated in Puerto Rico on 10th July.

Ingredients:
25ml white rum
75ml pineapple juice
25ml coconut cream
Pineapple wedge/maraschino cherry
Crushed ice

Place all of the ingredients in a blender with a handful of crushed ice. Blend until smooth, then pour into a chilled poco grande glass and garnish with a wedge of pineapple or a maraschino cherry.

39

DRINK RUM. DRINK RUM.
DRINK RUM. BY GUM WITH ME.
I DON'T GIVE A DAMN
FOR ANY DAMN MAN.
THAT WON'T TAKE A DRINK WITH ME.

Anon

OVERPROOF RUM

A rum is said to be overproof if it has an ABV of above 57%. When sailors were issued rum rations, they used to test its strength by mixing it with gunpowder. Any rum with an ABV lower than 57% would make the gunpowder too wet so that it would fail to light, and the sailors would know that their ration had been watered down, making it 'underproof'. To calculate the 'proof' of a spirit, just double the ABV, so for example, Bacardi 151 proof has an ABV of 75.5%.

I PITY THEM GREATLY, BUT I MUST BE MUM, FOR HOW COULD WE DO WITHOUT SUGAR AND RUM?

William Cowper

IT WAS HOT RUM PUNCH ... IT FILLED THE SOUL WITH WELL-BEING; IT DISPOSED THE MIND AT ONCE TO UTTER WIT, AND TO APPRECIATE THE WIT OF OTHERS; IT HAD THE VAGUENESS OF MUSIC AND THE PRECISION OF MATHEMATICS.

W. Somerset Maugham

SPLICE THE MAINBRACE

When sailors were ordered to perform the skilled and dangerous task of repairing the longest line of all – the running rigging (splicing the mainbrace), they would be rewarded with extra rum rations, so the term has long been associated with getting drunk at sea.

REASSURINGLY EXPENSIVE: HALL OF FAME

Only 1,000 hand-made crystal decanters of Havana Club Máximo Extra Añejo are produced every year, and each sells for about £1,250. It is a blend of rare and high-quality Cuban rums from the distiller's reserves, crafted by Maestro Ronero, Don José Navarro. Its aroma includes smoky and oak notes, and the taste includes fresh pear, coconut, dried fruit and vanilla with a warm spicy finish.

THE MOST SALUTARY LIQUOR

In 1762, in *An Essay on the Most Effectual Means of Preserving the Health of Seamen in the Royal Navy*, Dr James Lind wrote that rum 'is the most salutary Liquor than can be contrived to answer the Purpose [as a sovereign remedy]; besides its immediate cooling, refreshing and invigorating Quality, it is, in the Whole, well adapted to prevent the Diseases arising from hot and moist Weather, and the Tendency to Corruption in the animal Juices, which is thence supposed to be induced'. He even devised his own rum punch recipe, using fruits or fruit juice, vinegar-based shrubs, cream of tartar, a half-pint of spirits and a half-pint of water.

THE WORLD'S STRONGEST

Clarke's Court rum has been produced in Woodlands Valley in the southern part of the island of Grenada since 1937. Their Pure White Rum (69% ABV) is made from molasses, and blended to produce this seven-time International Gold award winner. Clarke's Court Spiced Rum (69% ABV) is aged for a year in ex-whisky barrels, and is infused with local spices.

ALL ROADS LEAD TO RUM.

W. C. Fields

THE BEST IDEAS COME WHILE SIPPING RUM.

Pavol Kazimir

HOW TO MAKE A HURRICANE

The Hurricane is a cocktail made with rum, orange and passion fruit juice, and it is very popular in New Orleans, where it is traditionally served in a tall curvy 'hurricane glass'. It is thought to have been invented in the 1940s by New Orleans tavern owner Pat O'Brien.

Ingredients:
50ml dark rum
50ml white rum
50ml passion fruit juice
25ml orange juice
15ml freshly squeezed lime juice
1 tbsp simple syrup (equal parts water and sugar)
1 tbsp grenadine syrup
Maraschino cherries
Orange slice

Shake all ingredients in a cocktail shaker with crushed ice and strain into a hurricane glass filled with more ice. Garnish with a cherry and an orange slice.

MOUNT GAY

The world's oldest commercial rum distillery is Mount Gay Distilleries Ltd. in Barbados, the easternmost island of the West Indies, whose oldest surviving deed is from 1703 as the Mount Gilboa Plantation/Distillery. The company changed its name in 1801 in honour of the recently deceased Sir John Gay Alleyne, a baronet and Barbadian politician who owned and ran the operation from 1747. He was admired as a businessman and philanthropist. He was also one of the first owners to speak out against slavery.

PRODUCT PLACEMENT

In *Casino Royale* (2006), the first drink James Bond (Daniel Craig) orders is not his trademark vodka martini but a Mount Gay rum with soda.

I CAN'T SIT IN A CORNY PLACE LIKE THIS COLD SOBER. CAN'TCHA STICK A LITTLE RUM IN IT OR SOMETHING?

Holden Caulfield, *The Catcher in the Rye*

|||||||||||||||||||||||||||||||||||||||||||||||||||||||||||||||||||||||||||||||||||||||||||||||||||||||||||||||||||||

REASSURINGLY EXPENSIVE:
HALL OF FAME

Bacardi-Millennium was created to celebrate the new millennium. Just 3,000 bottles (Baccarat crystal decanters) were produced from Cuban rum that had been aged in sherry casks for eight years. Originally retailing at US$500, today each bottle fetches in excess of US$2,500.

I WONDER WHETHER THEY HAVE RUM AND COKE® IN HEAVEN? MAYBE IT'S TOO MUNDANE A PLEASURE, BUT I HOPE SO – AS A SUNDOWNER. EXCEPT, OF COURSE, THE SUN NEVER GOES DOWN THERE. OH MAN, THIS HEAVEN IS GOING TO TAKE SOME GETTING USED TO.

Desmond Tutu

RUM VOTES

By the middle of the eighteenth century, rum was easily available and very popular among American colonists, who were consuming nearly four gallons a year per person. Politicians even used rum on the campaign trail. When George Washington ran for the Virginia House of Burgesses in 1758, he dished out 28 gallons of rum and 50 gallons of rum punch to secure goodwill. Also, his famous Mount Vernon eggnog packed a punch with its dark Jamaican rum.

51

I'M DRINKING LOTS OF RUM AND POPPING PINKS AND GREYS.

L. Ron Hubbard (founder of Scientology)

HOW TO MAKE A MOJITO

Mojito is a traditional Cuban highball with five ingredients: white rum, lime juice, sugar, soda water and mint. Some sources trace its origins back to a sixteenth-century drink called 'El Draque' after the English sea captain and slave trader, Sir Francis Drake. Its name probably relates to *mojo*, a Cuban seasoning made from lime.

Ingredients:
45ml white rum
6 leaves of mint
soda water
30ml freshly squeezed lime juice
2 lime wedges
2 tsp sugar

Put the lime wedges in a highball glass, then add sugar and freshly squeezed lime juice, and muddle together. Bruise the mint leaves by slapping them on the palms of your hand, then rub around the rim of the glass, drop them in and muddle again. Half fill the glass with crushed ice, pour in the white rum and stir. Top with crushed ice, a splash of soda water and garnish with mint leaves.

ONLY IN HAITI, I REALISED, IS IT POSSIBLE TO DRINK RUM AND HAGGLE WITH A GOD.

Wade Davis, *The Serpent and the Rainbow*

MAN'S MONOPOLY

In 1784. Mr James Man – who ran a sugar cooperage and brokerage – was awarded the exclusive contract to supply rum to the Royal Navy. His company retained this monopoly right up until 'Black Tot Day' when the tot of rum was abolished on 31st July 1970. Consistent quality was paramount, so Man became one of the first people to blend rum commercially, drawing supplies from all over the Caribbean and blending them in huge Solera-style vats at the Royal Navy Victualling Yard on the south bank of the Thames at Deptford.

I KNOW NOT WHY WE SHOULD BLUSH TO CONFESS THAT MOLASSES WAS AN ESSENTIAL INGREDIENT IN AMERICAN INDEPENDENCE. MANY GREAT EVENTS HAVE PROCEEDED FROM MUCH SMALLER CAUSES.

John Adams

REASSURINGLY EXPENSIVE:
HALL OF FAME

The daily ration of British Royal Navy Imperial Rum to sailors in the Royal Navy was stopped on 31st July 1970, leaving vast quantities of reserve rum, which was then transferred from barrels into wicker-clad stone flagons. These stocks remained the property of the Admiralty until Mark Andrews, a Texan oil investor, purchased 650 of the flagons and made them available to the general public for US$3,000 each.

> I FANTASISE ABOUT TENNESSEE WILLIAMS' TYPES OF EVENINGS INVOLVING RUM ON THE PORCH ... I FANTASISE ABOUT BEING CREDIBLE. IN THAT ARTISTIC, SLIGHTLY BOHEMIAN WAY THAT ONLY GIRLS WITH VERY LONG LEGS CAN GET AWAY WITH.
>
> Amy Mowafi

THE WORLD'S STRONGEST

John Crow Batty Rum is 80% ABV. 'They call it John Crow Batty because you had to have a stomach as strong as the John Crow vultures to drink it', says Paul Harris, managing executive at Hampden Estate in Trelawny, Jamaica. This is where sugar cane has been grown since 1753, and where the rum is produced today using pristine mountain rainwater. The estate also produces Rum Fire Overproof (63% ABV), one of the best Jamaican overproof rums.

I LIVED ON RUM, I TELL YOU. IT'S BEEN MEAT AND DRINK, AND MAN AND WIFE, TO ME.

Robert Louis Stevenson

NELSON'S BLOOD

Rum has acquired many nicknames: Kill-devil, Barbados Water, Demon Water, Pirate's Drink, Navy Neaters, Screech. On 21st October 1805, Horatio Nelson was mortally wounded as he commanded the British Navy to victory against French and Spanish fleets at the Battle of Trafalgar. It was customary to throw dead bodies overboard, but Nelson's body was preserved in a cask of brandy for the long journey back to England from the southwest coast of Spain. By the time his body reached home, the rumour spread that the soldiers guarding Nelson's body had drunk most of the 'rum' in his casket (they hadn't, and it was brandy not rum), but it was too late – the rumour persisted, earning rum the gruesome nickname 'Nelson's Blood', and having a sneaky drink became known as 'tapping the Admiral'.

|||||||||||||||||||||||||||||||||||||||||||||||||||||||||||||||||||||||||||||||||||||||||||||||||||

HOW TO MAKE A MISSIONARY'S DOWNFALL

—

Created by Don Beach in the 1930s at his beachcomber-themed restaurant in Hollywood, California, USA, the Missionary's Downfall is one of the most popular Tiki cocktails of all time (his version used pineapple chunks and a blender).

Ingredients:
60ml white rum
15ml peach schnapps
45ml freshly squeezed lime juice
60ml pressed pineapple juice
15ml sugar syrup
12 mint leaves

Bruise the mint leaves by muddling them in the base of the shaker. Add all of the ingredients plus crushed ice, and shake well. Strain into a Collins glass with ice and garnish with a mint leaf.

DRINKIN' RUM BEFORE 10:00 AM MAKES YOU A PIRATE, NOT AN ALCOHOLIC.

Earl Dibbles Jr.

RUM, N.
GENERICALLY, FIERY LIQUORS THAT PRODUCE MADNESS IN TOTAL ABSTAINERS.

Ambrose Bierce

RUM REBELLION

The Rum Rebellion of 1808 was the only successful armed takeover of the government in Australian history. After his overthrow from the mutiny on the Bounty, William Bligh became the Governor of New South Wales. Even before his arrival, the deeply unpopular Bligh managed to fall out with one of his subordinates, and sent him back to England to be court-martialled. Soon after his arrival at Sydney in August 1806, Bligh banned the use of spirits as a means of payment, which was a progressive policy designed to help the poor settlers, but it angered the rich traders. This policy, combined with his heavy-handed authoritarian rule of the colony, made Bligh many enemies among the rich and powerful. One notable enemy was the British army officer and entrepreneur John Macarthur, who overthrew Bligh by force with the New South Wales Corps after marching to his house, where they supposedly discovered 'cowardly' Bligh, hiding behind his bed. The uprising only became known as the Rum Rebellion many years later, when a teetotal English Quaker, William Howitt published a history of Australia, in which he named the incident the Rum Rebellion, gave an account that was favourable to Bligh and blamed the conflict on the evils of drink.

‖‖

HOW TO MAKE A CABLE CAR

—

The original Cable Car cocktail was created in 1996 by Tony Abou-Ganim at the Starlight Room nightclub in San Francisco, USA.

Ingredients:
50ml spiced rum
25ml Giffard Orange Curaçao
15ml freshly squeezed lemon juice
1 tsp sugar syrup

Fill a cocktail shaker with ice, add all the ingredients, shake well and strain into a chilled cocktail glass.

OF ALL THE HOT LIQUORS, I REGARD BUTTERED RUM AS THE WORST. I BELIEVE THAT THE DRINKING OF IT SHOULD BE PERMITTED ONLY IN THE 'NORTHWEST PASSAGE' AND EVEN THERE, ONLY BY HIGHLY IMAGINATIVE AND OVERENTHUSIASTIC NOVELISTS.

David A. Embury

WHAT IS YOUR BIGGEST ADULT FAILURE TO DATE? BE HONEST. DID IT INVOLVE COCONUT-FLAVOURED RUM? IT DID, DIDN'T IT? OH, COCONUT RUM.

Kelly Williams Brown

> MOST MEN, IT SEEMS TO ME, DO NOT CARE FOR NATURE AND WOULD SELL THEIR SHARE IN ALL HER BEAUTY, AS LONG AS THEY MAY LIVE, FOR A STATED SUM — MANY FOR A GLASS OF RUM. THANK GOD MEN CANNOT AS YET FLY, AND LAY WASTE THE SKY AS WELL AS THE EARTH!
>
> Henry David Thoreau

REASSURINGLY EXPENSIVE:
HALL OF FAME

The title of most expensive rum in the world is held by four remaining bottles of J. Wray & Nephew Rum from the 1940s, which are worth about US$54,000 each. The company was founded by John Wray in 1825 in Kingston, Jamaica, and remains one of the most successful businesses on the island today. This was the original rum called for by Trader Vic for his famous Mai Tai (see page 19).

BACARDI

Today, the largest rum distillery in the world is still in the Caribbean – it is the Bacardi distillery in San Juan, Puerto Rico, which produces 100,000 litres every day and is known as the 'cathedral of rum'. Bacardi Ltd. is the largest privately held, family-owned spirits company in the world. Founded in Cuba in 1862 by a Spanish wine merchant Facundo Bacardi Massó, it has been family-owned for seven generations. The founder filtered his rum through charcoal and aged it in white oak barrels to produce the world's first white rum. Fruit bats nesting in the rafters in his distillery became the inspiration for the famous bat logo. Today, the company has more than 200 brands and labels, and sells more than 200 million bottles per year.

DON'T YOU FEEL LIKE A LITTLE GLASS OF RUM? IT'S CUBAN, LIKE ALL THE GOOD STUFF THAT KILLS YOU.

Carlos Ruiz Zafón

MELTING POT HARLEM–HARLEM OF HONEY AND CHOCOLATE AND CARAMEL AND RUM AND VINEGAR AND LEMON AND LIME AND GALL.

Langston Hughes

BACARDI VS FIDEL CASTRO

A century later, during the Cuban Revolution, the Bacardi family initially supported and funded Cuban revolutionaries, including Fidel Castro, but their support turned to opposition. On 15th October 1960, the Castro regime seized all of the company's assets, as well as its production plant at Santiago and started producing the national rum – Havana Club – in that very building. However, loyal staff destroyed the unique yeast culture which made Bacardi, and smuggled a small amount to Puerto Rico, where it was free to grow into the global force it is today.

> WHEN I DIE, BURY ME DEEP WITH A SIX-PACK OF BEER BETWEEN MY FEET, A FIFTH OF LIQUOR AND A BOTTLE OF RUM. I'LL RAISE HELL TO KINGDOM COME.
>
> Chris Barton

|||||||||||||||||||||||||||||||||||||||||||||||||||||||||||||||||||||||||||||||||||||||||||||||||||||||||||

HOW TO MAKE A
CUBA LIBRE

Cuba gained independence from the US in 1902, and this cocktail – 'Free Cuba' – was born around this time. American troops introduced Coca-Cola® into Cuba in 1900.

Ingredients:
1 lime, cut in half
50ml dark rum
Ice
Coca-Cola®

Add freshly squeezed lime juice into a highball or Tom Collins glass, then add some lime peel and muddle it around in the juice for a minute. Remove the peel, add ice, dark rum and top up with Coke®. Garnish with a slice of lime. For the best flavour, purists advise using generic South American cola made with sugar rather, than America Coca-Cola® which is made with corn syrup.

I'M GETTING A HEADACHE. WINE MAKES MY HEAD EXPLODE. WHERE'S THE RUM AND COKE?

Julia Lednicky

I WAS HUNGRY AND WENT OUT
FOR A BITE. RAN INTO A CHUM
WITH A BOTTLE OF RUM AND WE
WOUND UP DRINKING ALL NIGHT.

Jimmy Buffett

THE WORLD'S STRONGEST

The Stroh Rum brand is one of the best-known spirits from Austria. Despite its 80% ABV, Stroh 80 Rum manages to offer an intense mixture of rich spicy aromas and tastes, with a woody nose and caramel-like sweetness, the taste notes of potpourri and butterscotch, and a long musty finish with nutmeg and cloves.

MY LAST FIVE YEARS OF DRINKING WAS A NIGHTMARE. I WAS DRINKING A HALF-GALLON OF RUM WITH A FIFTH OF RUM ON THE SIDE, IN CASE I RAN OUT, 28 BEERS A DAY AND THREE GRAMS OF COCAINE JUST TO KEEP ME MOVING AROUND. AND I THOUGHT I WAS DOING FINE BECAUSE I WASN'T CRAWLING AROUND DRUNK ON THE FLOOR.

Dennis Hopper

||||||||||||||||||||||||||||||||||||||||||||||||||||||||||||||||||||||||||||||||||||||||||||||||||||||||||||||||

REASSURINGLY EXPENSIVE: HALL OF FAME

Ron Bacardi de Maestros de Ron, Vintage, MMXII was created to mark Bacardi's 150th year anniversary, using 40 of the finest blends, created over time by eight Bacardi Master Blenders and rested for 20 years in 60-year-old Cognac barrels. Each numbered hand-blown crystal decanter priced at US$2000 has a walnut stopper, leather case and explanatory booklet. The rum has a full-bodied blend of tastes from honeyed tropical fruit, crème caramel and dark chocolate to coffee beans, smoky sandalwood and dried prunes, with a spicy finish of cinnamon and nutmeg.

CLOUDLESS SKY ABOVE MY HEAD
A MUG OF RUM IN MY HAND
CHAOTIC MESS IN MY HEAD
WHICH IS GETTING CLEAR
ON EACH SIP I TAKE.

Reikanin Palabo

I ORDERED ANOTHER RUM ST. JAMES AND I WATCHED THE GIRL WHENEVER I LOOKED UP, OR WHEN I SHARPENED THE PENCIL WITH A PENCIL SHARPENER WITH THE SHAVINGS CURLING INTO THE SAUCER UNDER MY DRINK.

Ernest Hemingway

DON'T WORRY ABOUT NEGATIVE TEMPERATURES BECAUSE MINUS TIMES MINUS EQUALS PLUS. IF YOU ARE NOT VERY GOOD AT MATHS, THEN PUT SOME RUM IN THE TEA.

Ljupka Cvetanova

HOW TO MAKE A DARK 'N' STORMY

This cloudy golden cocktail has been credited to members of Bermuda's Royal Naval Officer's Club, who added a splash of the local rum to their homemade ginger beer.

Ingredients:
50ml dark rum
25ml freshly squeezed lime juice
1 candied ginger slice
100ml chilled ginger beer
Lime wheel

Fill a cocktail shaker with ice, add the rum and lime juice, and shake well. Strain into an ice-filled highball glass and gently stir in the ginger beer. Garnish with the candied ginger slice and lime wheel.

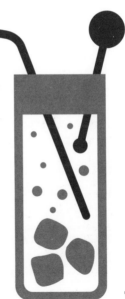

CURE FOR BALDNESS

In the 1800s, many people used rum to clean and thicken their hair, and some even believed it prevented hair loss. Rubbing a strong rum onto the scalp might improve blood flow to the region and offer marginal protection, so it is not as crazy as it sounds.

> I LEARNED HOW TO ORGANISE INTENSELY, HERE. I LEARNED THE PASSION. I LEARNED HOW TO DRINK A LOT OF PUERTO RICAN RUM. I HAD A BLAST. IT WAS GREAT.
>
> Jeb Bush

I'M IN THE MOOD TO GET NUMB ... IF I WANTED TO GET DRUNK I'D BE DRINKING STRAIGHT FROM A RUM BOTTLE.

Amanda M Lee

ANGEL'S SHARE

The liquid which evaporates through porous wooden casks during maturation is known as the Angel's Share, which is usually around 2% of the contents per year. It can be as much as 8% a year during the ageing of tropical rum, due to the climate.

CARIBBEAN RUM DOESN'T HAVE THE SAME AROMA **AS RUM FROM MAURITIUS, MAURITIAN RUM IS SHAPED BY NATURE.**

Alain Bouton

REASSURINGLY EXPENSIVE:
HALL OF FAME

Legacy by Angostura was launched in 2012 to mark the 50th year of independence for Trinidad and Tobago, with a limited run of 20 bottles. It was created as a blend of the company's 'rarest and most precious rums', and was presented in a crystal decanter designed by Asprey of London, jeweller to the Prince of Wales, with an 'elaborately-designed stopper that took 10 master craftsmen 560 hours to complete' in Sterling silver. Three bottles were released in the US and sold for US$25,000 each, and just two went on sale in Harrods in London for £20,000 each.

PINK ELEPHANTS

In 1982, an army ordinance corps in Bagdogra in eastern India hit the news for fighting a losing battle against thieving elephants. On several occasions, elephants had emerged from the thick forest close to the Bangladesh border to ransack the army rations stores to steal food and drink. The soldiers noted that the elephants had a particular fondness for 96 proof army rum; there were even reports of an elephant reaching through a window with his trunk and lifting out a 12-bottle crate. According to an eyewitness report in *The Daily Telegraph*, the elephants broke the rum bottles by curling their trunks around the base, 'then they would empty the contents down their throats. They soon got drunk ... and swayed around. They enjoyed themselves and then returned to the jungle'.

THE TASTE IS SUGAR-CANE, SLOWLY ROTTING, TURNING INTO THE GREAT GOD RUM.

Pavol Kazimir

THE WORLD'S STRONGEST

The second strongest commercially available rum in the world is Sunset Very Strong Rum, an 84.5% product of Saint Vincent, distilled from molasses in a column still. It is crystal clear, and the Ministry of Drinks describes its taste as 'warm like sweet butter, with secondary flavours of citrus/meyer lemon, coconut and mild vanilla. The medium body is reminiscent of white chocolate, leading nicely to a dry, short, buttery finish'.

RUM IS TONIC THAT CLARIFIES THE VISION, AND SETS THINGS IN TRUE PERSPECTIVE.

Brian D'Ambrosio, *Fresh Oil, Loose Gravel*

HOW TO MAKE AN EL FLORIDITA

This is essentially a Daiquiri (see page 11) prepared with Maraschino liqueur, the way Ernest Hemingway used to order it at the Floridita bar in Havana, Cuba.

Ingredients:
50ml white rum
25ml freshly squeezed lime juice
15ml Maraschino liqueur
Wedge of lime

Fill a cocktail shaker with ice, add the rum, lime juice and Maraschino, and shake well. Strain into a chilled cocktail glass and garnish with a lime wedge.

THE **ONLY WAY** THAT I COULD FIGURE THEY COULD IMPROVE UPON COCA-COLA® — **ONE OF LIFE'S MOST DELIGHTFUL ELIXIRS,** WHICH STUDIES PROVE WILL **HEAL THE SICK AND OCCASIONALLY RAISE THE DEAD** — IS TO PUT RUM OR BOURBON IN IT.

Lewis Grizzard

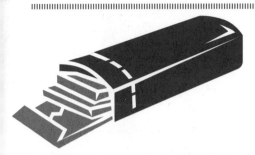

CHEWING GUM MORE FATAL THAN RUM?

The genius Serbian inventor, Nikola Tesla, maintained a strict diet of mainly milk, water and vegetables and rarely ate meat, but he considered alcohol to be a 'veritable elixir of life'. He found US prohibition (1920–1933) very tough. On 10th August 1932, he published an article in support of drinking in the *New York World Telegram* titled 'Chewing Gum More Fatal Than Rum'. He argued that chewing gum 'by exhaustion of the salivary glands, puts many a foolish victim into an early grave'. The article was even more scathing about tea and coffee, particularly for women, as 'a means of committing beauty suicide', however, 'the truth about alcohol is that it acts as a caustic and a solvent. In small quantities, it cleans and sterilises the alimentary channels, thereby preventing infections, and proves a beneficial stimulant to thought, speech and physical exertion'.

THERE'S NAUGHT, NO DOUBT, SO MUCH THE SPIRIT CALMS AS RUM AND TRUE RELIGION.

Lord Byron

REASSURINGLY EXPENSIVE:
HALL OF FAME

In 2013, to coincide with the company's 125th anniversary, Brugal released 500 crystal decanters of Papà Andrés rum (named after the founder, Don Andrés Brugal), priced at US$1,200 each. The rum was taken from the private Brugal family reserves, some of which was more than 100 years old. 'Papà Andrés is a rum which has evolved through the passion, care and expertise of five generations of master blenders, all of whom have been members of my family', said Franklin Báez Brugal, Brugal president.

> THE FIRST TIME I PLAYED THE MASTERS, I WAS SO NERVOUS I DRANK A BOTTLE OF RUM BEFORE I TEED OFF. I SHOT THE HAPPIEST 83 OF MY LIFE.
>
> Chi Rodriguez

THE WORLD'S STRONGEST

At 90% ABV, the strongest commercially available rum in the world is Mariënburg, produced in Suriname, the smallest country in South America. The company that produces it – Suriname Alcoholic Beverages (SAB) – was formed in 1966 by several local distributors. Its now defunct sugar factory was built in 1882 by the Netherlands Trading Society, and the Mariënburg sugar cane plantation dates back to 1745. Today, all of the processing takes place in Paramaribo.

TIME FLIES WHEN YOU'RE HAVING RUM.

Erik Voskamp

93

HOW TO MAKE
RUM PUNCH

There are lots of versions of Rum Punch, but the IBA
Official Cocktail Planter's Punch (with dark rum, several
juices, grenadine syrup, sugar syrup and Angostura bitters)
originated at the Planters Hotel in Charleston, South
Carolina, and the recipe appeared in the September 1878
issue of the London magazine *Fun*:

> A wine-glass with lemon juice fill,
> Of sugar the same glass fill twice
> Then rub them together until
> The mixture looks smooth, soft, and nice.
> Of rum then three wine glasses add,
> And four of cold water please take. A
> Drink then you'll have that's not bad –
> At least, so they say in Jamaica.

Ingredients:
45ml dark rum
35ml fresh orange juice
35ml fresh pineapple juice
20ml fresh lemon juice
2 tsp grenadine syrup
2 tsp sugar syrup
3 dashes Angostura bitters
Maraschino cherries
Pineapple wedge

Mix all of the ingredients, except the bitters, into a cocktail shaker filled with ice. Shake well and strain into large highball glass, filled with ice. Add Angostura bitters, and garnish with a cocktail cherry and pineapple slice.

HOW TO MAKE SPICED RUM. PLACE RUM, ALLSPICE, CLOVES, CARDAMOM, STAR ANISE, CINNAMON, NUTMEG, ORANGE PEEL AND ONE VANILLA BEAN – SPLIT LENGTHWISE – IN A JAR, AND STORE IN A DARK PLACE FOR TWO DAYS. STRAIN RUM USING CHEESECLOTH. POUR AND ENJOY.

Ellery Adams

RUM MAKES A FINE HOT DRINK, A FINE COLD DRINK, AND IS NOT SO BAD FROM THE NECK OF A BOTTLE.

Fortune magazine, 1933